IMAGES
of America

CHARLESTON
A HISTORIC WALKING TOUR

Fulton St.

205 Meeting St.

Market St.

Archdale

King St.

Church St.

Orange

Meeting St.

Legare St.

King St.

Atlantic St.

South Battery

South Battery

MAP. This map shows the routes of the Meeting Street and Legare Street tours narrated in this book. You are encouraged to follow your own path, though, using the book for reference and information. A tour should be an adventure in discovery and understanding. The old city is on a peninsula, so getting too lost is not an option without getting wet. Each tour lasts about two hours and is a circle that starts and ends at the Charleston Place Hotel at 130 Market Street, where there is a parking garage. There are several house tours offered on the Meeting Street circuit that take 20 or 30 minutes each. Using this map, you can see where the tours can be divided if you prefer to take it in smaller bites. You could also drive to a halfway point, but walking is truly the best way to see the city. Keep in mind that there are real families making homes in these houses, and respect their property and privacy. Places where there are possible public restrooms are marked with an RR.

ON THE COVER: Cover photo taken by Ronald Allen Reilly in Washington Park. The girl on the left in the photograph is Katherine Reynolds Manning. The girl on the right is her sister Betsey Reynolds Robinson. If you can identify the girl in the middle please contact the author at bitsyf@gmail.com.

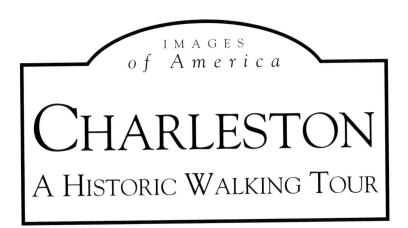

IMAGES
of America

CHARLESTON
A HISTORIC WALKING TOUR

Mary Preston Foster

ARCADIA
PUBLISHING

Published by Arcadia Publishing
Charleston, South Carolina

Printed in the United States of America

Library of Congress Catalog Card Number: 2004117437

For all general information contact Arcadia Publishing at:
Telephone 843-853-2070
Fax 843-853-0044
E-mail sales@arcadiapublishing.com
For customer service and orders:
Toll-Free 1-888-313-2665

Visit us on the Internet at www.arcadiapublishing.com

VIEW FROM ST. MICHAEL'S STEEPLE. This photograph was taken from St. Michael's Steeple before 1886 looking north on Meeting Street. The building in the right foreground is the Fireproof Building with the skylight over the stairway visible. In the center are the burned-out remains of the Circular Church, missing its domed roof. Its steeple is missing two tiers. On the left is the Mills House Hotel. The steeple in the distance on the left is St. Matthew's German Lutheran Church built in 1872. (South Carolina Historical Society Collection.)

CONTENTS

ACKNOWLEDGMENTS

Ann Tiller encouraged me through the process of putting this book together. Adam Latham was the editor at Arcadia who made it sound simple and made it all pleasant. My brother, John Cantzon Foster, Ph.D., has done the genealogy for our family back to John of Og, including all of the allied families. His work broadened the scope of this considerably. Vickey Colson at Charleston Place was the key to my tour guide business. David Kelly at the South Carolina Department of Archives and History was most helpful with pictures of the Ansonborough area. Mike Coker helped with the ones from the South Carolina Historical Society. Mrs. Roulain DeVeaux was most generous with the pictures taken by her grandfather, George Johnson. The Library of Congress American Memory website provided many of the pictures; I mourn that I couldn't use the picture of chickens on Tradd Street, but some of the best pictures were just not reproducible. All of the facts in this book are documented, but there could be errors in that documentation. The broad sweeping conclusions are my own and could be argued. Please contact me (BitsyF@gmail.com) or the publisher with any comments.

MEETING STREET IN RUINS, 1865. This photograph of Meeting Street was taken looking south with St. Michael's Church in the center. The Circular Church is on the left with its tower in scaffolding. The building on the right is the Mills House Hotel. The destruction is the result of the fire of 1861 and the bombing by United States forces during the Civil War.

INTRODUCTION

When our country was begun, the Virginia colony was founded by political dissenters deeply dissatisfied with the government in England. The political rabble-rousers in the creation of this nation came from Virginia. We owe our reverence for liberty and distrust of government to them. New England was founded by people seeking religious freedom. Their government, through the church, controlled all aspects of daily life. We owe our "big government" tendencies to those founders. In contrast, South Carolina was founded by individual adventurers. The people who founded this colony in 1670 mostly came from England, some by way of the West Indies. The French Huguenots came as a group, but the rest came because land was cheap and the potential for profit was great. They came with the idea of re-creating the society of England on a higher level than they could hope to achieve in England. Titles such as Landgrave and Cassique were offered, depending on the number of servants and acres of land. Individual people came to South Carolina looking for a good life, and for many, that's what they found. Is it any wonder that it was the people of South Carolina who "got rich" first and had the first theater, the first lending library, the first museum, the first city college, the first opera performance, and the first golf club? The state was hot, and the emphasis was on entertainment, culture, and business. The plantations were large and isolated, and transportation was dusty and difficult. Large landowners had town houses and spent a part of each year in town to escape the tropical diseases as well as to conduct business. South Carolina's political interest lay in the effect of politics on business and economic issues.

The first significant wealth derived from the Indian trade and then the planting of rice and indigo. Plantations on tidal water and a large cheap labor force were necessary for success, so slaves were imported from the parts of Africa where rice was grown. The wealthy of the 1700s traveled and educated their sons in England and set a standard for luxurious living and conspicuous wealth. South Carolina had the highest per capita income on the continent before the Revolution. Gabriel Manigault (1758–1809), a merchant, was thought to have been the wealthiest man in America, proving that the planters were not the only people benefiting. Rice was successfully planted until about 1908, but after the Revolutionary War, South Carolina lost the trade advantage given to rice and indigo by the British. The invention of the rice mill by Jonathan Lucas in the 1790s helped keep it profitable. This industry, along with the culture and society of the various social classes, produced much of the history that Charleston enjoys today.

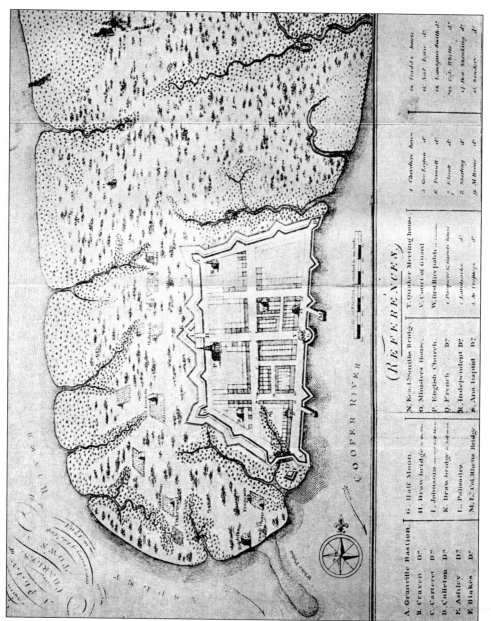

CRISP'S MAP. At the direction of the Lords Proprietors, Charles Town, as the city was known until after the Revolutionary War, was laid out in what was called the Grand Modell. This map made by Edward Crisp in 1704 shows that a wall had been constructed around the most populated part of the peninsula. The inland wall corresponds to Meeting Street from First Scots Church to Cumberland Street and the outer wall corresponds to the area from the Missroon House to Water Street. By 1720, the Native Americans and the pirates had been defeated and the Spanish threat had subsided. The colonists were becoming more numerous and more prosperous, and the walls began to come down as the settlement expanded across the peninsula. Creeks and waterways were filled in, but they tend to revert to type in heavy rains. Every election promises to solve the water problems downtown. (From *Narratives of Early Carolina, 1650–1708*, edited by Alexander S. Salley Jr.)

Tour One

MEETING STREET LOOP
Meeting Street, the Battery, and Church Street, Including St. Michael's and St. Philip's Churches

This walk takes you through the oldest part of the city with the oldest houses and the most important public buildings. Four of the houses are open for tours for a small fee. The predominant style of the 1700s was the single house, which is only one room wide to allow cool air to circulate to all of the rooms. Usually, a piazza across the front provides shade, and the ceilings are high and the windows large to further assist in cooling. The ends of the houses face the street with a door that leads not into the house but onto the piazza. The front door is in the center of the piazza and leads to a stairhall with a room on each side on every floor. Considering that many of these families had ten or more children, that is not really very many rooms. If the house is on a busy street, the parlor is usually found on the second floor to escape the noise and dirt of traffic. (Horses did not wear diapers then.) Because of frequent fires, it became a law that kitchen buildings had to be made of brick and placed ten feet from the main house. Besides the kitchen, each house had a carriage house and stable and other dependencies that still exist. Servants' quarters were on the second floor of these buildings.

CHARLESTON PLACE HOTEL, 130 MARKET STREET. All of these tours begin and end here. This hotel was built in the 1980s, replacing a row of commercial buildings that looked much like the ones still standing on the rest of the block. It has shops and restaurants and a beautiful staircase. There is a parking garage at the Hasell Street entrance through the lobby.

MARKET HALL, 188 MEETING STREET. The United Daughters of the Confederacy have recently completed a restoration of this building and maintain a Confederate museum inside. This was built as a meat market in 1841, evidenced by the rams and bulls heads in the frieze. The market that stretches behind Market Hall was a produce market where people were allowed to sell their vegetables, shrimp, and baskets; it was never used as a slave market. It is said that in earlier times, wagons lined up for miles along Meeting Street as farmers brought their crops to sell here. The name Charleston Eagles was given to the flocks of buzzards that plagued the area enjoying the refuse. They were protected by law.

CIRCULAR CONGREGATIONAL CHURCH, 150 MEETING STREET. This Romanesque Revival church is the fourth one on this site and was completed in 1892 using bricks salvaged from an earlier structure. It replaces a circular church, designed by Robert Mills, built in 1804, which burned in the fire of 1861. This church is tri-apsidal or fan-shaped. The original congregation, formed in 1681, included French Huguenots, Congregationalists, Scots, and Irish Presbyterians, or anyone not wishing to be affiliated with the Church of England. As these groups gained members, they broke away to establish separate congregations. In 1968, this church became affiliated with the United Presbyterian Church. The first church on this site was called the White Meeting House and gave Meeting Street its name.

11

LANCE HALL, 138 MEETING STREET. On the grounds is the parish house and Sunday school for the Circular Church. Services were held in this building while the church was being renovated. Lance Hall was built in 1867 and is typical of the Roman Revival buildings of that time. It is one story built over an aboveground basement.

CEMETERY. The oldest graves in Charleston are found in this cemetery. It has an interesting variety of grave styles, reflecting the mix of the congregation. There are broken columns and obelisks as well as mausoleums. The death's heads are reminiscent of the Congregational cemeteries found in New England. The elegance of the tombstones attests to the wealth of the people of earlier times.

THE GIBBES MUSEUM OF ART, 135 MEETING STREET. James Shoolbred Gibbes (1819–1888) bequeathed the money to establish an art museum and school. This building was completed in 1904 in the Beaux Arts style and replaces the Grand Opera House that burned in 1894. The focus of the collection is local artists and portraits. It has one of the oldest collections in the country.

MR. AND MRS. RALPH IZARD. This 1774 portrait done by John Singleton Copley of Mr. and Mrs. Ralph Izard of Charleston shows great wealth and sophistication. Owned by the Boston Museum of Fine Art, it has been on loan to the Gibbes. Raised on the Elms plantation, Ralph was educated in England and served in the Continental Congress and the United States Senate.

13

MILLS HOUSE HOTEL, 115 MEETING STREET. Today, the Mills House is a modern and successful hotel. In 1853, Otis Mills, a grain merchant, built the most luxurious hotel that $200,000 could build. It was in the Italianate style and elegant in every detail with steam heat and running water. The balcony was made of cast iron from Philadelphia, and the window details were ordered from Massachusetts. In 1861, when fire ravaged the neighborhood, the employees hung wet blankets from the windows and saved the hotel. Robert E. Lee was a guest at the time. The building was replaced in 1968 in the same style, using the old balcony and recasting the window details. The new structure has two more floors than the previous one.

HIBERNIAN SOCIETY HALL, 105 MEETING STREET. The Hibernian Society was formed in 1801 as a benevolent group to support Irish immigrants. This hall was built in 1840. The stone on the portico was brought from the Giant's Causeway in County Antrim, Ireland, in 1851. Notice the Irish harps in the door panel and gates, and the owl in the window.

INSIDE THE HIBERNIAN. Inside, there are large halls upstairs and down, perfect for dancing on one floor and serving food on the other. The proper Charleston debutante gets married in St. Michael's or St. Philip's and has her reception at the Hibernian or the South Carolina Society Hall. This is the site of the St. Cecelia Society balls and an annual St. Patrick's Day celebration.

FIREPROOF BUILDING, 100 MEETING STREET. This building was designed by Robert Mills and was completed in 1827 in the Greek Doric style. Mills was born in Charleston and studied architecture under James Hoban and Thomas Jefferson. He was the first native-born American architect. This is now the home of the South Carolina Historical Society and houses items related to South Carolina history. (George Johnson.)

INSIDE THE FIREPROOF BUILDING. An oval stone staircase is cantilevered for three stories inside and lit by a skylight. Mills's original design for the Washington monument is here and shows the obelisk surrounded by buildings that look like the Fireproof. They only built half of his design. A replica of the monument is in the courtyard. Non-members are allowed to use the library for research for a small fee.

CHALMERS STREET. The cobblestones in Chalmers Street were used as ballast in the ships coming from England during the Colonial period. Sometimes bricks were used; a brick expert examining one of Charleston's walls claimed to have found Elizabethan bricks in it imported in that way. A wagon ride down Chalmers Street was once said to induce the birth of babies.

WASHINGTON PARK. The statue of George Washington and the name of this park commemorate the visit he made to Charleston in 1791. He came to honor the fact that there were more battles of the Revolutionary War fought in South Carolina than any other state. This statue of William Pitt was erected around 1766 to honor his part in having the Stamp Act repealed. It is now in the county courthouse. A confused child once said it was George Washington just getting out of bed. (George Johnson.)

CITY HALL, 80 BROAD STREET. Designed by Gabriel Manigault, City Hall was built in 1801 of red brick and white Italian marble in the Adamesque style. Built as a branch of the Bank of the United States, it became City Hall in 1818, after the bank lost its charter. The red bricks were covered with stucco in an 1882 renovation. Free tours are offered. (RR.)

INSIDE CITY HALL. This photograph of the council chambers was taken after the 1882 renovation. The portrait of George Washington on the back wall was painted by John Trumbull in 1791. There was a dispute with the artist, so he added the horse in the background with his rear end foremost. Other portraits include Samuel F.B. Morse's rendering of James Monroe and Charles Fraser's miniature of Lafayette.

COUNTY COURT HOUSE, 77 MEETING STREET. Charles Town was the state capital until 1786 when Columbia was made the capital to appease the upcountry citizens. The state house was built on this site in 1752, and when it burned in 1788, this building was constructed using the foundation and what walls remained of the prior building. It was renovated in 1883 and the 1990s.

POST OFFICE AND FEDERAL COURT HOUSE, 83 BROAD STREET. This Renaissance Revival building was completed in 1896 to replace a guard house (police station) that was destroyed by the earthquake of 1886. This structure was designed by Charleston architect John Henry Devereaux to resemble an Italian palace. The sword gates from the guard house are at the Citadel and a private home at 32 Legare Street. (RR.)

ST. MICHAEL'S EPISCOPAL CHURCH, 80 MEETING STREET. This church was completed in 1761 and is credited to an Irish architect, Samuel Cardy. It is thought to be one of the finest Georgian churches in the United States. The steeple was targeted by the gunboats bombarding the city from 1863 to 1865, and this photograph shows that some of the shells hit their mark. In the earthquake of 1886, the building settled eight inches, necessitating a step up in the vestibule. The clock and bells came from England in 1764, were removed during the Civil War, and were sent to Columbia for safekeeping, where they were burned by General Sherman. After being sent to England for recasting, they were reinstalled in time for the earthquake. Just eight days after the earthquake, when the steeple was separated from the church and people were still camped in Washington Park, the sexton climbed the steeple and tolled the bells. A wooden casket with "JOB" and "1675" in nails on the cover was found encased under the steeple stairs. If the doors are open, you are welcome to go in. (South Carolina Historical Society.)

INSIDE ST. MICHAEL'S. The octagonal pulpit was in place in 1761 with its inlaid mahogany sounding board. The baptismal font dates from 1771 and has a lead dove pulley for lifting the lid. The chandelier is English and dates to 1803. The Governor's Pew (number 43) was used by George Washington in 1791 and by Robert E. Lee in 1862.

ST. MICHAEL'S PARISH HOUSE AND CEMETERY, 80 MEETING STREET. The tombstone of James Lewis Pettigru, a Unionist, is on the back wall behind the grave of Robert Y. Hayne. President Woodrow Wilson read Pettigru's epitaph at the conference that ended World War I, noting, "He withstood his people for his country, but his people did homage to the man who held his conscience higher than their praise." (The epitaph was not published by this point, so Wilson must have seen it in the cemetery.) John Rutledge and Charles Cotesworth Pinckney, signers of the Constitution, are also buried here. The bedstead tombstone of Mary Ann Luyten is in the front corner.

ST. MICHAEL'S RECTORY, 76 MEETING STREET. The ghost of a dying duelist haunted this house until it was purchased by St. Michael's. There was bumping on the stairs as his limp body was carried up. The house was once owned by Judge Bay; in 1819, he presided over the hanging of the first woman in South Carolina. She, Lavinia Fisher, had killed travelers in her tavern, called Six Mile House.

SOUTH CAROLINA SOCIETY HALL, 72 MEETING STREET. The South Carolina Society was formed by French Huguenots in 1737 as a charity called the "Two Bit Club." The society established schools for the poor until public schools began. This Adamesque building dates from 1804 and was designed by Gabriel Manigault, who was a member of the group. The lantern stands date from the 1760s.

POYAS HOUSE, 69 MEETING STREET. This classic single house has an Adamesque interior and was built between 1796 and 1800 by Dr. John Ernest Poyas Jr. The blue ceilings on the piazzas were supposed to discourage insects. A later owner, Moses Cohen Mordecai, financed the retrieval of the bodies of South Carolina soldiers killed in the battle at Gettysburg.

PRIOLEAU HOUSE, 68 MEETING STREET. This house was built in 1810 as a single house by John Cordes Prioleau. In the 1890s, William Bachman Chisolm purchased it with money made in the manufacture of phosphate fertilizer. It was remodeled to add Victorian and Queen Anne embellishments, but the single house bones are still discernible.

HASELL HOUSE, 64 MEETING STREET. Andrew Hasell, a planter, built this single house *c.* 1788. He was the grandson of Rev. Thomas Hasell, who was the first minister of Pompion Hill Church in Berkeley County. Letters from Reverend Garden to Lord Ashley give detailed accounts of the character and actions of all Episcopal ministers of the Proprietary Era. Copies reside with the South Carolina Historical Society.

BRANFORD-HORRY STABLE, 61 MEETING STREET. The stable of the Branford-Horry house was adapted in 1913 to a respectable two-story home. It was the home of Federal District Judge J. Waties Waring, who declared in 1947 that the South Carolina Democratic Party was not a social club and thus could not hold political primaries that excluded black voters. Notice the tile roof.

BRANFORD-HORRY HOUSE, 59 MEETING STREET. Built in 1751, this double house with a magnificent Georgian interior was built by William Branford, a planter, as his town house. His grandson, Elias Horry, lived here when he was president of the South Carolina Railroad, which had the longest rail in the world in 1833; it ran from Charleston to Hamburg (near North Augusta).

ELLIS HOUSE, 60 MEETING STREET. The core of this house was built as a double tenement by William Ellis c. 1771. The Victorian remodeling was done by Bertram Kramer, a bridge and wharf builder and general contractor. It once had a roof garden where the family entertained.

FIRST SCOTS PRESBYTERIAN CHURCH, 57 MEETING STREET. This church was organized in 1731 by 12 Scottish families. This building dates from 1814 but the cemetery is older. Henry Erskine, the third Baron Cardross, founded a settlement of Scots south of Charleston in 1684 called Stuarts Town. Resented by the English in Charleston and attacked by the Spanish and Native Americans, the settlement lasted only two years.

NATHANIEL RUSSELL HOUSE, 51 MEETING STREET. Nathaniel Russell, a Rhode Island merchant, spent $80,000 on this Adamesque house before 1809. It was saved from demolition in 1955 by the Historic Charleston Foundation, which has used it for offices ever since. It is open for tours and has a gift shop in the garden. (RR.)

BARNWELL HOUSE, 47 MEETING STREET. This photograph was taken in 1938 when this house was being used as a business. It is an antebellum single house that was home to Edward Barnwell, a factor and planter who grew prize fruits and vegetables in his garden. He had 17 children, and it is said that he added on to the back of the house several times to accommodate them.

BEAUREGARD'S HEADQUARTERS, 37 MEETING STREET. Built in 1760 by James Simmons, this structure was bought by Gov. Robert Gibbes in 1760. When the British occupied Charleston in 1781, they vandalized the house. In 1861, it was the home of Otis Mills, who offered it for Beauregard's use. It is said to have pirate treasure buried in the yard and a pirate ghost that guards it.

WILLIAM BULL HOUSE, 35 MEETING STREET. This was built in 1720 as the town house of William Bull, a rice planter. When the colonists rebelled against the Lords Proprietors and formed a Royal Colony in 1729, William was selected to be the lieutenant governor representing the colonists to the royal governor appointed by the king. He was succeeded by his son, who was also named William.

DANIEL HUGER HOUSE, 34 MEETING STREET. This Georgian house was built about 1760 and was the home of the last royal governor, Lord William Campbell, who fled under revolutionary threat in 1775. He escaped using a creek that ran from the backyard to the harbor. Except for a few years up until 1818, the house has remained in the Huger family.

ISAAC MOTTE HOUSE, 30 MEETING STREET. Isaac Motte purchased this house in 1770, and his descendants owned it for 147 years. After the Revolution, Motte allowed Hessian officers who did not want to return on the British ships to hide in the broad chimneys. Motte served as a colonel in the Patriot army and was a planter on the Cooper River.

WILLIAM MASON SMITH HOUSE, 26 MEETING STREET. The son of the first Episcopal bishop, Rt. Rev. Robert Smith, built this Regency house c. 1822. Some attribute it to Robert Mills. The three tiers of piazzas have columns in the classic order; Doric, Ionic, and Corinthian. The interior has a curving stair, and a later owner added an elevator.

HEYWARD HOUSE, 18 MEETING STREET. Thomas Heyward, signer of the Declaration of Independence, built this house soon after 1803. His plantation was in St. Luke's Parish. The house has an Adamesque interior with carved moldings and marble mantels. Thomas helped draft the South Carolina Constitution in 1776. He was imprisoned in St. Augustine during the British occupation. His plantations were in the Beaufort District.

CALHOUN MANSION, 16 MEETING STREET. George W. Williams built this Victorian mansion in 1876. Williams was a successful merchant before the Civil War and made $1 million during the war, some say as a blockade runner. The house is the largest home in the city, with 24,000 square feet and 25 rooms. The ballroom upstairs has a 45-foot ceiling with a glass skylight. Tours are offered. (George Johnson.)

EDWARDS HOUSE, 15 MEETING STREET. John Edwards built this house in 1770 using cypress boards cut and beveled to look like stone. The Georgian interior is one of the best in the city. A later owner, George Williams Jr, son of George W. Williams, added the semi-circular piazzas to accommodate the children from the orphanage for ice cream parties.

TUCKER-LADSON HOUSE, 8 MEETING STREET. James Henry Ladson, a factor and planter, added the front portion of this house to one built by Capt. Thomas Tucker before 1783. James was the son of Maj. James Ladson. They descended from an English Quaker who came to South Carolina in 1679. Members of the Ladson family occupied this house until 1961. (George Johnson.)

CARRINGTON-CARR HOUSE, 2 MEETING STREET. George W. Williams's daughter, Martha, was given $75,000 when she married Waring P. Carrington and they built this Queen Anne house. There are three Tiffany windows in it that were gifts for their fifth wedding anniversary. It is said that Mr. Tiffany himself brought them from New York and oversaw their installation.

ROSS MUSEUM, 1 MEETING STREET. This Italianate house was built in 1846 by a cotton broker. In 1870, William Middleton sold it to the Ross family, which had a magnificent collection of art and antiques. When Miss Mary Jane Ross, the last of her family, died in 1922, she left the entire estate as a museum. A court battle ensued that lasted until 1944, ending with the house being sold and the money going to charities.

PAVILION, WHITE POINT GARDEN. The pavilion was a gift of Mr. and Mrs. Waring Carrington. It was used for free band concerts on Sunday afternoons for many years and is now a popular site for weddings. The park is shaded by oak trees and there is a constant breeze, which made this park a favorite place in the days before air conditioning.

SOUTH BATTERY. This photograph was taken from atop the Fort Sumter Hotel. Charleston's wars and heroes are commemorated in statues and weapons in this park. Children climb on the cannons, feed and chase the pigeons, and look for sharks' teeth in the oyster shell paths. Nannies and mothers bring babies in strollers, and couples come here to watch the "submarine races."

CANNON, THE BATTERY. During the Revolutionary War and then the Civil War, Charleston was under siege, and this park had fortifications all around what is now the sea wall; thus it was called the Battery. Charleston was occupied and defeated in both wars, but the city was taken by land. It has never been conquered from the sea.

FORTIFICATION, THE BATTERY. This Blakely cannon has been dismantled. In 1865, the city had been overrun and was under federal occupation that would last until 1876. These houses had been evacuated. The Defenders of Fort Sumter monument in the park is said to be the only insured monument in the United States.

ASHE HOUSE, 26 SOUTH BATTERY. This house in the Italianate style was built in 1853 for Col. John Algernon Sydney Ashe, a bachelor. The rooms on the end follow the rounded shape of the exterior and are decorated with ornate plasterwork. The house also features a curving stair.

STEVENS HOUSE, 20 SOUTH BATTERY. Built in 1843 by Samuel Stevens, this house was purchased and enlarged in 1870 by Richard Lathers. Lathers was born in Georgetown, South Carolina, moved to New York, and served in the Union Army. He entertained prominent Southerners with occupying officers to promote reconciliation. Failing, he returned to New York, selling the house to Andrew Simonds in 1874.

WILLIAM WASHINGTON HOUSE, 8 SOUTH BATTERY. When this house was built in 1768, it had a Church Street address, probably because there was no street where South Battery is now and no White Point Garden. William was George Washington's younger cousin who came to fight the Revolutionary War in South Carolina, married Jane Elliott, and stayed. (George Johnson.)

VILLA MARGHERITA, 4 SOUTH BATTERY. This 1895 mixed-style house replaced a pre-Revolutionary single house. It was operated as a European "pension," a forerunner of the bed and breakfast, and hotel from 1914 to 1953. Henry Ford and Alexander Graham Bell were among its guests. Since 1961, it has been a private home.

FORT SUMTER. Cross the street to walk on High Battery. The island directly in the center of the harbor is Fort Sumter. On April 12, 1861, Citadel cadets at Fort Johnson on James Island fired on the fort to oust Major Anderson and his federal troops. South Carolina had failed in its attempt to buy all federal installations within her borders, and these troops were a threat to her sovereignty. (South Carolina Historical Society.)

EAST BATTERY. Mary Boykin Chesnut watched the bombing of Fort Sumter from one of these roofs with General Beauregard, while her husband carried the messages between Beauregard and Anderson by rowboat. When a bomb burst, she swooned, landing on the chimney and setting her dress on fire. Her writings of the Civil War are wonderfully real.

DeSaussure House, 1 East Battery. Thomas Coffin, a planter, built this modified single house in 1850 and sold it to Louis DeSaussure in 1858 for $7,500. The house was damaged by the earthquake of 1886, and the iron balconies were added in the renovation. One of the owners was Mrs. Mary Middleton Pinckney Lee, wife of Col. Robert E. Lee III, who was a grandson of the Confederate hero.

Ravenel House, 5 East Battery. Dr. St. Julien Ravenel lived in this house built by his father in 1849. Dr. Ravenel was a physician who developed the use of phosphate rock as fertilizer, an artesian well water supply, and with David Ebaugh, built a semi-submersible torpedo boat. His wife was Harriet Horry Rutledge, who wrote *Charleston: The Place and the People* in 1906.

ROPER HOUSE, 9 EAST BATTERY. Built in 1838, this was the first house constructed on East Battery. It was designed by Edward Brickell White for Robert William Roper. When Charleston was overtaken by Sherman's troops, a Blakely cannon was blown up, and a fragment of it lodged between the rafters, where it remains. Robert was married to the daughter of Henry Laurens, and they had no children. His bequest founded Roper Hospital. (George Johnson.)

WILLIAM RAVENEL HOUSE, 13 EAST BATTERY. William Ravenel, a shipping merchant, built this house in 1845. The Tower of the Winds columns were lost in the earthquake of 1886. The capital of one of the columns was found when hurricane Gracie uprooted a tree in 1959 and the capital was exposed under its roots. (South Carolina Historical Society.)

EDMONSTON-ALSTON, 21 EAST BATTERY. Charles Edmonston immigrated from Scotland, purchased a wharf at Exchange Street, and made a fortune. He built this Regency house in 1828 and sold it to satisfy creditors in 1838. Charles Alston, who bought it, was the son of one of the wealthiest planters in the state. He added the Alston Coat of Arms on the parapet. The house is open for tours.

DRAYTON HOUSE, 25 EAST BATTERY. Charles H. Drayton of Drayton Hall Plantation built this house in 1885 with profits from mining phosphate. It is unusual with its Medieval and Chinese architectural details and its use of white stone with black grout, which has been hidden under stucco. His plantation house is said to be a fine example of Georgian architecture and is open for tours.

PORCHER-SIMONDS HOUSE, 29 EAST BATTERY. Francis Porcher, a cotton broker and president of the Atlantic Phosphate Company, built this house in 1856 in the Italianate style. When John C. Simonds bought it in 1894, he added the front piazzas and the wing on the left side. He was the president of the First National Bank, which he sold in 1926.

NATHANIEL INGRAHAM HOUSE, 2 WATER STREET. Born in Boston, Nathaniel came to Charleston with the U.S. Navy. His son, Duncan, was a hero of the U.S. Navy until he resigned to join the Confederate Navy, where he distinguished himself. Duncan married the granddaughter of Henry Laurens, president of the Continental Congress. The house was built in 1810 and remodeled in the 1870s.

East Bay St. near the Battery. Charleston - S.C. mch-1895.

MISSROON HOUSE, 40 EAST BATTERY. Capt. James Missroon purchased this house on the water side of the battery from Harry Grant, who built it in 1789. It was converted to a hotel in 1905 and then enlarged to become the Omar Shrine Temple in 1925. A part of Granville Bastion was found during the renovation. Albert Simons designed the temple addition behind it. (South Carolina Historical Society.)

BENJAMIN SMITH, 1 ATLANTIC STREET. Cross the street to enter Atlantic Street at the Drayton House at 25 East Battery. This house is on the left. The structures at both 1 and 3 Atlantic were built in 1830 by Benjamin Smith, a shipbuilder. In the 18th century, both Charleston and Georgetown had shipbuilding facilities. Number 3 Atlantic was the childhood home of Elizabeth O'Neill Verner, the artist.

WATT'S GROCERY, 26 CHURCH STREET. The house at the corner of Church and Atlantic Streets was built between 1794 and 1796. James Watt purchased it in 1796, lived upstairs, and operated a grocery store on the first floor. Atlantic Street was widened and moved in 1800, putting this house, which had been two doors down, on the corner.

JAMES H. ANCRUM HOUSE, 20 CHURCH STREET. To see this house, you must turn left at the corner of Atlantic and Church Streets onto the brick surface. James Ancrum inherited the William Rhett house, sold it, and lived here by 1809. He was married to a daughter of Col. William Washington. The house was owned by William Holmes from 1795.

CARRIAGE HOUSE, 19 CHURCH STREET. Number 19 was built as the carriage house for the Calhoun mansion in 1875 and converted to a home in 1939 by architects Simons and Lapham. Eighteenth- and nineteenth-century interior embellishments were installed. This is one of the few remaining brick-surfaced streets in the city.

THOMAS YOUNG HOUSE, 35 CHURCH STREET. Thomas Young built this house *c.* 1770, the same time as the house at 30 Meeting Street on the same lot. It became the home of Dr. Joseph Johnson, physician, author, mayor, and bank president. Dr. Johnson's father was a blacksmith who led the Mechanics in protesting the Stamp Act. Joseph wrote *Tradition of American Revolution* describing events of that time.

VANDERHORST-MATTHEWS HOUSE, 37 CHURCH STREET. Constructed between 1743 and 1750, this property was owned by Maj. John Vanderhorst, a ship captain for whom Vanderhorst Creek was named. He sold it to Anthony Matthews in 1743. It is said that Vanderhorst kept his gold in a water keg on his front piazza where it remained safe. The Vanderhorst family came from Rotterdam, Zuid, Holland.

EVELEIGH HOUSE, 39 CHURCH STREET. Built in 1743 by George Eveleigh, an Indian trader, this Georgian house is one of the most photographed in Charleston. The original grant included the property at 34 Meeting Street, and in 1775, when the last royal governor abruptly left that house, he came through this yard to a boat on the harbor. The cement posts are for tying up boats.

THOMAS YOUNG HOUSE, 14 WATER STREET. This house was built in 1769 by Young, the same person who later constructed the house at 35 Church Street. It faced Vanderhorst Creek, which was filled in to create Water Street. There is a Mutual Insurance Company marker on the Church Street side. Jacob Motte is said to have founded the first fire insurance company in Charleston in 1736.

52 CHURCH STREET. This pre-Revolutionary single house seems to be nameless. The unrenovated look makes an excellent reference for comparison. Stoll's Alley is on the right. Number 7 Stoll's Alley was built in 1745 by a blacksmith, Justinus Stoll, from whom the alley gets its name. The alley leads to East Battery.

55 CHURCH STREET. Notice that this pre-Revolutionary single house has no piazzas, typical of this style. The vine around the doorway is Confederate jasmine, distinguished from the yellow jasmine, the state flower, by its tiny white flowers. In the 1960s, this house was made up of apartments with one large room divided to make two. The interior still has its original carved crown moldings.

THOMAS ROSE HOUSE, 59 CHURCH STREET. The ghost of Dr. Joseph Ladd Brown, who died here after being wounded in a duel over an actress in 1786, haunts this house. It was built in 1733 with an entry in the center. A later owner bought and razed the house next door, adding the piazzas and a garden.

FIRST BAPTIST CHURCH, 61 CHURCH STREET. The Baptist congregation came from Kittery, Maine, with Rev. William Screven in 1682. This church is the second on this property donated by William Elliot. It was designed by Robert Mills and dedicated in 1822. This is the mother church of all Southern Baptist congregations. Behind the church, there is a private school that incorporates the Adger House at 68 Meeting Street.

INSIDE FIRST BAPTIST CHURCH. The Baptist congregation was persecuted in Maine, and when Reverend Screven removed his church to South Carolina, there was not another Baptist church in Maine for 85 years, according to Harriott Ravenel. By the early 19th century, the Baptists were only outnumbered by the Episcopalians. This part of Church Street was called Baptist Town.

CAPERS-MOTTE HOUSE, 69 CHURCH STREET. One of the largest private homes in the city, with a second-floor drawing room that spans the entire width of the house, this house was built by Richard Capers in 1745. Jacob Motte, the king's treasurer, raised 20 children here, 18 by his first wife and 2 by his second, making him a progenitor of most old South Carolina families.

ROBERT BREWTON HOUSE, 71 CHURCH STREET. This is thought to be the earliest surviving single house in the city, built perhaps as early as 1721. Robert Brewton inherited the land from his father, Miles, and built this house. He was a wharf owner, militia officer, and member of the Commons House of Assembly. The formal garden was designed by Loutrel Briggs. It is a registered National Historic Landmark.

CHURCH STREET. Sixty-nine Church Street is the first house on the left of this photograph, which faces north toward St. Philip's Church. This was taken in the very early 1900s in a time of transition. Notice the posts to tie horses on a street with cars and an electric pole beside a house with a gas lantern at the door. (George Johnson.)

TRADD STREET. This block of Tradd Street is two blocks past the corner of Church; the photograph was taken from the opposite direction at the same time as the one above. During Reconstruction, the phrase "too poor to paint and too proud to whitewash" described the dilemma of homeowners. These photographs show just how long that condition lasted for some Charlestonians. (George Johnson.)

BREWTON'S CORNER, 77 CHURCH STREET. The Brewtons at one time owned 71, 73, 77, and 79 Church Street as well as 35 and 38 Tradd Street; thus the name of this home. The present house was built around 1810 by Louis Danjou as a grocery store with his residence above. Number 75 was his warehouse and stable. Col. Robert Brewton's son, Miles, built the mansion at 27 King Street.

BEDPOST HOUSE, 78 CHURCH STREET. Two houses have been combined to make one here. Dubose Heyward, who wrote *Porgy and Bess,* lived here in the 1920s, and George Washington is said to have spoken from the balcony when he visited in 1791. The third floor was found to be supported by a mahogany bedpost during a renovation; it was left in place.

ELIZABETH O'NEILL VERNER'S STUDIO, 38 TRADD STREET. To your left on Tradd Street, this house was built between 1718 and 1722 by John Bulloch. Inside is a tiny house believed to date from 1670 before the settlement moved to the peninsula from Charles Towne Landing. It is the office seen straight back from the front door. It was two stories but the stairs were outside.

TENEMENT, 41–43 TRADD STREET. Jonathan Badger built this tenement c. 1746. The metal circles lined up between the second and third stories are earthquake bolts. They are attached to metal rods that run through the house with corresponding bolts on the other end. These were put in after the earthquake of 1886 to hold the walls together. They can be seen in various forms in houses built before 1886.

COLEMAN FINE ART, 79 CHURCH STREET. Elizabeth O'Neill Verner lived in this three-house complex (combining the house within 38 Tradd with 38 Tradd and 79 Church) from 1938 until she died in 1979. This was one of the houses Robert Brewton acquired in his marriage to Millicent Bulloch. Millicent was exiled to Philadelphia during the British occupation because of her quick-witted barbs to British officers.

HENDRICKS TENEMENT, 83–85 CHURCH STREET. William Hendricks, a planter, built this double tenement in 1749. It was meant to be two separate residences, so the kitchen building in the back was also double. The kitchen is now a third separate residence and can be seen through the archway.

HEYWARD-WASHINGTON HOUSE, 87 CHURCH STREET. Daniel Heyward, a rice planter in St. Luke's Parish, built this house around 1770 after removing a previous house. Thomas Heyward, his son and signer of the Declaration of Independence, inherited it and had George Washington as his houseguest for a week in 1791. It is a double house with a wide center hall. In 1883, Arthur Mazyck wrote that this house is "no longer in a fashionable part of the city." Mrs. Ravenel's book of 1906 shows it with an awning and says it is a bakery. The house was restored by the Charleston Museum and the Preservation Society in 1929 and is now open for tours. Thomas later lived at the house on Meeting Street.

THOMAS ELFE MANTEL, 87 CHURCH STREET. Thomas Elfe was a master cabinet and furniture maker, thought to be the best in Charleston in the 18th century. His house and shop are at 54 Queen Street. This is a 1930s photograph of the second-floor drawing room of 87 Church showing the mantel and other woodwork. (George Johnson.)

STABLE, 87 CHURCH STREET. It is believed that when Daniel Heyward removed the previous house on this site, he kept all of its outbuildings; this assumption is made because these buildings date from an earlier time and are made of earlier brick than the main house. The outbuildings are furnished and give an excellent view of the work required to keep people fed and clothed in the 18th century.

CABBAGE ROW, 89–91 CHURCH STREET. Dubose Heyward renamed this double tenement Catfish Row in his story "Porgy." Built before the Revolution, it had become a bordello in the 1880s. African Americans moved in after that, sold cabbages and other produce downstairs, and lived upstairs and in the alley. Loutrel Briggs, the landscape architect, restored it in the 1920s.

ALEXANDER CHRISTIE HOUSE, 92 CHURCH STREET. This Adamesque single house was built about 1805 by a Scottish merchant, Alexander Christie. When the first floor was a business, the middle window was a door. This has been the rectory for St. Philip's Church since 1908.

NULLIFICATION HOUSE, 94 CHURCH STREET. This house was built around 1760. It was owned by Gov. Joseph Alston in 1830 when Robert Y. Hayne and John C. Calhoun met with him here to write the Ordinance of Nullification; this established that any state could nullify any federal law within its borders. Governor Alston was married to Theodosia Burr, daughter of Aaron Burr, who was lost at sea.

VICTORIAN ROW, 93–99 CHURCH STREET. This row of Victorian houses was built around 1910, replacing the Charleston Hydraulic Cotton Press Company. These houses make it possible to say that Church Street has magnificent examples of almost every architectural style from the Colonial period to the 1900s, including residential and commercial structures.

THE HAT MAN, 47 BROAD STREET. The hat man painted on the Church Street side of this building dates from the late 1800s. The building was constructed in 1855 by two saddlers and harness makers and sold to Charles Plenge in 1870. Shephard's Tavern was located at 46 Broad Street from the early 1700s and was the hub of political and social activity.

BANK OF SOUTH CAROLINA, 50 BROAD STREET. This T-shaped building was constructed in 1797 as the Bank of South Carolina. In 1802, a would-be thief lived three months underground as he tunneled his way to the vault. His accomplice, who was supplying him with food and water, became careless, and they were both caught. It has housed the Charleston Library Society and the Charleston Chamber of Commerce.

PAUL HOUSE, 49 BROAD STREET. Benjamin Smith built this around 1740 as a business with living quarters upstairs. Dunbar Paul bought it in 1819 and had a grocery store on the first floor until 1901. It has Georgian paneling in the living quarters. The wrought-iron balcony is considered one of the best examples of 18th-century ironwork in the city.

OLD EXCHANGE AND PROVOST DUNGEON, 122 EAST BAY STREET. On the right at the end of Broad Street is the Old Exchange, built between 1767 and 1771. It was the site of a ball for Washington in 1791. Its dungeon housed Isaac Hayne, Christopher Gadsden, and other Patriots during the British occupation from 1780 to 1782. Isaac Hayne is the only person on record hanged as a traitor to the British during the Revolutionary War. Tours are offered. (RR.)

CHICORA ANTIQUES, 102 CHURCH STREET. This is an excellent example of an 18th-century building with a business on the first floor and family living quarters above. The residential entryway is on the side of the building and leads to an elegant home with fine Georgian molding and architectural embellishments.

ISAAC HOLMES HOUSE, 107 CHURCH STREET. Isaac Holmes built this three-story brick and stucco house after a fire in 1740 destroyed a previous residence. The interior has Georgian paneling and carved woodwork. On September 10, 2004, it was listed for sale for $1,750,000. The son of a Boston tavern owner, Isaac moved to South Carolina in 1721, married Elizabeth Peronneau, and became a successful merchant and planter.

SLAVE MART MUSEUM, 6 CHALMERS STREET. The Old Slave Mart Museum is housed where Z.B. Oakes erected this "shed" for slave auctions in 1859. The arch was enclosed with an iron gate leading to a large open room. The German Fire Company was built in 1851. The home at 34 Chalmers was built in 1835 for Jane Wightman, a free black woman. (South Carolina Historical Society.)

PINK HOUSE, 17 CHALMERS STREET. Toward the right on Chalmers is a brick and Bermuda stone stucco building built between 1694 and 1712 by John Breton. It was a tavern in Colonial times. It seems that Shepherd's Tavern on Broad Street was respectable, while this was referred to as the "sailors' tavern." Its tile roof is original. Alice R. Huger Smith, the artist, used it as her studio.

FRENCH QUARTER, 134 CHURCH STREET. This area was called the French Quarter because many of the Huguenots built and lived here. When the Edict of Nantes was repealed in France, the Protestants emigrated; 45 came to Charleston in 1680 and many more followed. They became rice and indigo planters in the Santee area and on the Cooper River. Number 134 was the rectory of the Huguenot church.

DOCK STREET THEATER, 135 CHURCH STREET. The first theater in America was built on the Queen (Dock) Street side of this property in 1735. This is a reconstruction of that 18th-century theater using the old Planter's Hotel building, its courtyard, and outbuildings. The woodwork and plasterwork were salvaged from an 1802 Adamesque house. This was accomplished by the Works Progress Administration in 1935.

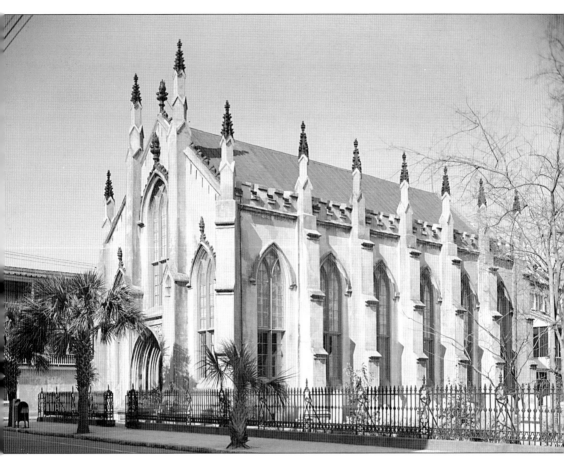

THE FRENCH HUGUENOT CHURCH, 136 CHURCH STREET. This church houses the only French Calvinist congregation in the United States since the one in New York joined the Episcopal Diocese. This Gothic Revival building was constructed in 1844. Ralph Izard donated the land, and Isaac Mazyck donated the money for the building of the first church in 1687. From 1680 to 1686, Huguenots arrived until they numbered about 450. Some of them had left France early enough to bring their wealth with them, but most came as poor refugees. Their rise to wealth and political power was rapid, and their influence was great in the social, political, and economic development of this state. The Huguenot Society of South Carolina is large and active. The first church on this site was blown up in an attempt to arrest the fire of 1796. It was called the "tidal church" because its services were timed with the tides to accommodate the planters coming by boat.

INSIDE THE FRENCH HUGUENOT CHURCH. Edward Brickell White was the architect for this, the first Gothic Revival church in Charleston. The vaulted ceiling is made of lath and plaster, and the exterior is of stuccoed brick. Many of the Huguenots joined the Episcopal Church, so this church ceased having services several times, the first time in 1823, but each time it is revived.

PIRATE HOUSES, 141–145 CHURCH STREET. The block of houses on the left have been called the Pirate Houses and are said to have a tunnel leading to the water through which they could escape. The stuccoed ones were built by Alexander Peronneau about 1740 using Bermuda stone and brick. Someone has written that Charleston was the favorite port of the pirates in the early 1700s.

St. Philip's Church, 146 Church Street. St. Philip's, organized in 1680, is Charleston's oldest Episcopal congregation. Its first church was built in 1681 on the site of St. Michael's. As that church aged, St. Philip's was begun on this site in 1710. It did not open for services until 1723, and the people had to bring their own chairs because the interior wasn't finished until 1727. When St. Michael's was completed in 1761, the congregation divided at Broad Street and people were compelled to attend the church designated by their address. In the great fire of 1796, St. Philip's was saved by an African-American boatman who climbed to the roof and threw off the burning shingles. He was given his freedom for his heroism. The church burned in the fire of 1835, and this church was built to be centered in the street like English churches built in the center of crossroads. George Washington attended services on his 1791 visit.

ST. PHILIP'S INTERIOR. Like St. Michael's, St. Philip's has boxed pews and an elevated pulpit. The pews were granted based on benevolent contributions and could be repossessed. The congregation wanted the new church in 1835 to be exactly like the old one but Joseph Hyde, the architect, replaced the Tuscan columns with the lighter Corinthian style.

ST. PHILIP'S GATES. The gates across the street date from 1770, and it is believed that these and the ones at the Miles Brewton house on King Street are the only wrought-iron gates to survive the pre-Revolutionary period. The gates surrounding the church date from 1826. They replace a brick wall that had gates with skulls and crossbones in them.

St. Philip's Graveyard. William Rhett, the pirate catcher, was buried here before the church was finished. Other illustrious people buried here include Edward Rutledge, signer of the Declaration of Independence, (who wrote his own epitaph and did not include that fact) and several Colonial governors. Across the street, the graveyard was used for strangers or people not born in Charleston. John C. Calhoun is buried there.

Powder Magazine, 79 Cumberland Street. This is the only public building that dates from the time of Proprietary rule. It was built for the storage of gun powder and was finished in 1713. It is one of the few buildings made of "tabby" that survive. It is now owned by the Society of Colonial Dames of America and is a museum open to the public.

CUMBERLAND STREET, 1865. This vision of the Archibald McLeish Vulcan Iron Works sign shows the range of iron works offered. The gates of Charleston are a testament to the talents of its iron workers of every era. Philip Simmons is a highly respected iron "artist" still working in the city.

MARKET BUZZARDS, 1865. This is it! You're back at the Market surrounded by places to sit down and rest your feet and talk about what you've seen. To your left is Market Hall at the end of the stalls and Charleston Place is right across the street. These are the buzzards mentioned at the start of this tour.

Tour Two

LEGARE STREET LOOP
Fulton, Archdale, and Legare Streets, the Battery, King Street, Orange Street, and Part of Broad Street

There is a distinct ambiance to each street in Charleston. It was interesting sifting through photographs and realizing that with some exceptions, the style and setting of a house indicated the street on which it was located. On the Meeting Street Loop, it seemed that the grown-ups lived on Meeting while the children lived on Church. In the same way, on the Legare Street Loop the grown-ups lived on Legare Street while the children lived on King. There is a house on Legare Street that dates from 1759 and one on King from 1765 so this idea is not based on age; it has more to do with the size of the lots and the attention paid to architectural details than antiquity. Also, while King and Broad Streets were both laid out as thoroughfares, Legare and Church were made up of little streets and lanes pieced together on land sometimes reclaimed from marshes and creeks. Orange and Fulton Streets are examples of alleyways that became streets, but in very different ways. That is made obvious on this 1788 map. (Library of Congress Maps Division.)

MAP, 1788. Edward Petrie published this map in 1788. (Library of Congress Maps Collection.)

69

RIVIERA THEATER, 225 KING STREET. Albert Sottile was the owner of this movie theater built in 1939. It replaced the Academy of Music that was built in 1869 for the performance of plays. Sarah Bernhardt performed there. It is said to be Charleston's best example of Art Moderne architecture. You will travel left on King Street for about one block.

MADAME PEIXOTTO'S HOUSE, 9–11 FULTON STREET. Just down King Street, you will turn right on Fulton Street. Both of the buildings on the left were built by Grace Peixotto in the 1850s and run as a bordello. It is said that a unit of Wade Hampton's Red Shirts was formed here while federal troops occupied the state. This event might have inspired a scene in *Gone With the Wind*.

PHILLIP PORCHER HOUSE, 19 ARCHDALE STREET. Fulton Street leads to Archdale, where you will proceed left. Phillip Porcher was a planter who cooperated with the British when they occupied the city. After the war, all Tories had their property confiscated. Many managed to get their property restored after a time. This house was built around 1773 and was eventually restored to the Porcher family.

ST. JOHN'S LUTHERAN CHURCH, 10 ARCHDALE STREET. There were Lutherans in the city as early as 1734, but the first congregation was organized in 1752. Dr. John Bachman was pastor from 1815 to 1874. He is known as the collaborator with John James Audubon on his *Birds of America*, and two of his daughters married two of Audubon's sons.

GATES OF ST. JOHN'S, 10 ARCHDALE STREET. The gates were designed by Abraham P. Reeves, a member of the congregation, and created by Jacob S. Roh in 1822. Reeves's brother-in-law, Frederick Wesner, was the architect of the church and also the Old Citadel. This is the home church of retired Sen. Ernest F. Hollings.

INSIDE ST. JOHN'S, 10 ARCHDALE STREET. The pulpit was donated by Jacob Sass. During the Revolutionary War, the minister of this church refused to pray for the King of England, had all of his property confiscated, and was expelled from the city by the occupying British. The church was badly damaged in the earthquake of 1886 and the hurricane of 1893.

UNITARIAN CHURCH, 6 ARCHDALE STREET. This church was completed in 1787. It was built to house the overflow of the Circular Congregational Church, and the two churches were one congregation with two ministers. In 1817, Anthony Forster, one of the ministers, declared himself a Unitarian and the congregation split with 69 remaining and 75 going with Reverend Forster. The assets were equitably divided.

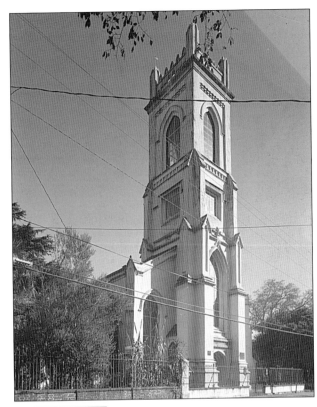

INSIDE THE UNITARIAN CHURCH, 6 ARCHDALE STREET. It is said that the British stabled their horses in this incomplete building during the occupation. In 1852, the building underwent extensive renovation that gave it its Gothic style. The fan-tracery was added to the vaulted ceiling at that time. The designer and renovation architect was Francis D. Lee. It is the oldest Unitarian church in the South.

UNITARIAN GRAVEYARD. This is the marker for the grave of Dr. Samuel Gilman, a graduate of Harvard University and minister from 1819 to 1858. He was the composer of "Fair Harvard," the school's alma mater. Gage Hall next door serves as the parish house and was donated by Alva Gage in 1893. It had living quarters on the second floor. Proceed to the end of Archdale Street.

CRAFTS HOUSE, 67 LEGARE STREET. You will take a slight jog to the right to arrive on Legare Street. Crafts House is now a condominium, but the building once housed a school named for William Crafts, a lawyer and advocate for free schools. It was built in 1881 in the Gothic Revival style to mimic an earlier school that burned in the fire of 1861.

CATHEDRAL OF ST. JOHN THE BAPTIST, 122 BROAD STREET. The first cathedral on this site, St. Finbar's and St. John's, was built in 1850, but it burned in 1861. The current structure was built between 1890 and 1907. It is said that each hour of work donated by a member of the church was rewarded with a star on the Connecticut brownstone bricks.

VALK HOUSE, 125 BROAD STREET. Construction on this house began in 1886 just before the earthquake hit, so when it was rebuilt, every effort was made to make it earthquake proof. The bricks are Stoney Landing bricks made locally. Charles Valk, born in Connecticut, was in school in Abbeville when the Civil War broke out; he volunteered for the Confederate Army at 16 with his classmates.

ELLIOTT HOUSE, 43 LEGARE STREET. Cross Broad Street and continue down Legare Street. Charles Elliott was a planter who built this house in 1759. His daughter made a flag for Col. William Washington's regiment when he passed their plantation in Eutaw Springs during the Revolution. She subsequently married him and, in 1827, presented that flag to the Washington Light Infantry organization.

BENNETT HOUSE, 37 LEGARE STREET. John Bennett of Ohio married Susan Smythe of Charleston, and her father gave them this house in 1903. John was an author of novels about Charleston, children's stories, and the first treatise on Gullah around 1905. Dubose Heyward, Hervey Allen, Josephine Pinckney, and Bennett founded the Poetry Society of South Carolina. The house was built *c.* 1818.

McCord House, 35 Legare Street.
This house was built before 1828 by
Rebecca Screven. It was purchased in
1879 by Mrs. Louisa McCord, daughter
of Langdon Cheves, who was one of the
most prominent women writers before the
Civil War. She ran a hospital for wounded
soldiers and raised a company for her son,
Cheves, who was killed. Her husband,
Edward, was an editor.

**Sword Gates, 32 Legare
Street.** Christopher Werner
made these gates in 1830 for
the Charleston Guard House.
Misunderstanding the order for
a "pair" of gates, the guard house
installed one set and Werner was
left with these until George Hopley
bought them in 1849 and installed
them here. The "swords" are the
horizontal lines. The Citadel
inherited the other pair from the
guard house. (George Johnson.)

SWORD GATE HOUSE, 32 LEGARE STREET. In 1828, Maria Whaley was sent to Madame Talvande's school here from her father's Edisto plantation to separate her from George F. Morris of New Jersey. She slipped out and they eloped, causing a scandal. Both the masonry and frame sections of the house were built before 1818. They became two residences in 1960 when the masonry section took the 111 Tradd Street address. (South Carolina Historical Society.)

SMYTHE HOUSE, 31 LEGARE STREET. Hannah Shubrick Heyward, a rice planter and widow of William Heyward, built this house in 1789. Her son, James, was killed in a hunting accident and appeared to her in the library at the moment of his death. His ghost still appears. Augustine T. Smythe, who spied on federal gunboats from a gas-filled balloon, bought the house in 1868, and his descendants still own it.

GERVAIS HOUSE, 29 LEGARE STREET. Rev. Paul Trapier Gervais built this house on a pre-Revolutionary foundation in 1835. He was the rector of the Episcopal church on Johns Island and opposed secession. In 1895, Josephine Pinckney, the author of *Hilton Head* and other novels and poetry, was born here. Her family maintained El Dorado, their rice plantation on the Santee.

WHALEY HOUSE, 26 LEGARE STREET. This Victorian house was built in 1895 by Judge Whaley to replace one that burned. The photograph shows the columned portico and Victorian details it had until it was remodeled by the present owner, T. Wilbur Thornhill, in 1937. The iron Xs on the front are earthquake bolts added to reinforce walls against earthquake damage. (George Johnson.)

CHISOLM HOUSE, 23 LEGARE STREET. Yes, Virginia, there really is a 23 Legare Street. Go down the driveway. Robert Trail Chisolm built this house *c.* 1838, but the iron gates date from 1817. His son, Dr. John Julian Chisolm, wrote *Chisolm's Manual of Military Surgery*, used in the Civil War. There was a ghost, but it left when the Chisolms sold the house.

GATEWOOD HOUSE, 21 LEGARE STREET. William C. Gatewood, a wholesale merchant from Virginia, built this house in 1843 and lived here until 1863. Gatewood was associated with the South Carolina Lottery. The house sold for $27,000 (Confederate dollars) in 1863, for $16,000 in 1927, and for $8,000 in 1942. During World War II, it was operated as an apartment and rooming house but is now a single family home.

FULLERTON HOUSE, 15 LEGARE STREET. During the British occupation from 1780 to 1782 this house was used by the British staff officers. It was built by a Scot, John Fullerton, c. 1772. He was a part of Christopher Gadsden's "Liberty Tree" gang that fomented the Revolution. In 1987, it became the first house in Charleston to sell for more than $1 million.

SIMMONS-EDWARDS HOUSE, 14 LEGARE STREET. This house was built in 1801 by Francis Simmons, a Johns Island planter. In a perversion of chivalry, he married Ruth Lowndes whom he felt had tricked him. On their wedding day, he took her to a home at 131 Tradd Street and returned here. A fatal duel was once fought between cousins in 14 and 15 Legare from third floor bedroom windows.

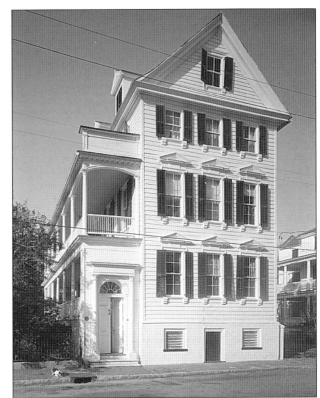

PINEAPPLE GATES, 14 LEGARE STREET. George Edwards bought the property in 1816, moving a house next door to create a walled garden. His initials are in the ironwork of the gates. He ordered live-oak acorns for his gates but the Italian marble carvers made "pinecones." In South Carolina, the pineapple is a symbol of hospitality so they became the "Pineapple Gates." (George Johnson.)

THURSTON HOUSE, 10 LEGARE STREET. Edward North Thurston built this Greek Revival single house in 1857 including the wall and wrought-iron gates. Notice the tropical flavor added by the use of palmetto trees in the landscape. Compare the photograph taken in the 1930s without the trees. The entryway to this house is an outstanding feature even without the portico.

MAYBANK HOUSE, 8 LEGARE STREET. This was the home of Burnet Rhett Maybank, mayor, governor, and senator. He died in 1954, paving the way for Strom Thurmond to join the senate, where he remained until 2003. It was built *c.* 1857 in the Italianate style. The builder is not known, but the contractor was Patrick O'Donnell for this house and 10 Legare.

MOVED HOUSE, 1 LEGARE STREET. This is the house that George Edwards removed from the lot beside 14 Legare in order to create his magnificent gardens. The story goes that it was put on rollers and rolled down the street to this location where it has remained. It was built before 1816.

DEPENDENCY, 51 1/2 SOUTH BATTERY.
This is a dependency of the much larger house at 51, perhaps the kitchen. It once had a decided lean to the right that has been largely corrected. Although often neglected in the literature, as is 51, this survivor is a worthy anchor to the splendor of Legare Street.

GIBBES HOUSE, 64 SOUTH BATTERY.
Just a half block to the right on South Battery, this pre-Revolutionary Georgian mansion is worth the detour. William Gibbes, a merchant, shipowner, and planter, built this house on the Ashley River with a wharf in front. The cove-ceilinged ballroom is considered one of the most beautiful rooms in America. One of the owners was Sarah Smith, whose descendants inherited Magnolia Plantation.

INSIDE 64 SOUTH BATTERY. In the 1920s, Mrs. Washington A. Roebling, widow of the man whose father built the Brooklyn Bridge, lived here. This is her drawing room. Notice that the carved door molding matches the mantelpiece. She improved the grounds by installing a garden that is included in the Harvard Survey of Design. Walk back down South Battery past Legare Street to King Street.

OSBORNE HOUSE, 56 SOUTH BATTERY. In *This Is Charleston*, Samuel Stoney describes this house as "a picturesque house devoid of pretentiousness." He also describes it as valuable. The house was built between 1783 and 1812, and it is believed that the ironwork was added in a later renovation. The name of the builder is unknown.

ENGLISH HOUSE, 49 SOUTH BATTERY. This house was built *c.* 1795 by Col. James English. There is an old sea wall in the rear of this property showing just how much marshland was reclaimed with fill. Edward Blake, William Gibbes, Robert Mackenzie, and George Kincaid worked together to accomplish this before 1800.

CHEVES HOUSE, 47 SOUTH BATTERY. Henry C. Cheves was a rice broker and president of a bank when he built this house in 1886. It was owned by Princess Pignatelli from 1930 to 1946. She was born Henrietta Pollitzer in Bluffton, South Carolina, and married first Edward Hartford and, after his death, Prince Guido Pignatelli of Italy. She bought the Joseph Manigault House and donated it to the Charleston Museum.

MAGWOOD-MORELAND HOUSE, 39 SOUTH BATTERY. Beneath this house is a bed of palmetto logs that give it flexibility. It was built by the Magwood family in 1827, and it is not known if it was built on the site of an old palmetto fort or if the builder conceived of this effective earthquake protection. Frank Lloyd Wright successfully used the concept in many of his structures.

HEINZ HOUSE, 36 SOUTH BATTERY. Frederick Heinz, a German baker, built this structure as his residence around 1889 and manufactured and operated the Battery Ice Cream Garden next door. This was the time of the free Sunday concerts at White Point Garden, and he was very prosperous. Eventually he built the houses at 38 and 40 as investments. Don't you wish it were an ice cream parlor now?

FORT SUMTER HOUSE, 1 KING STREET. On the water at the foot of White Point Garden stands what was once the Fort Sumter Hotel, built in 1923. It was the scene of wedding receptions and debutante parties and entertained rich and famous visitors to the city for 50 years. The hotel closed in 1974 and was converted to offices and condominiums.

INGRAHAM HOUSE, 10 KING STREET. Nathaniel Ingraham built this house *c.* 1791. He was a ship's captain who was born in Massachusetts and settled in Charleston after the Revolution. He volunteered to serve on the *Bonhomme Richard* under John Paul Jones and participated in his victory over the *Serapis*. He built 2 Water Street in 1810.

LAMBOLL HOUSE, 19 KING STREET. Thomas Lamboll bought this property and much that surrounds it in 1722 and built this house. His wife had the first flower garden in town. That is a wonderful symbol of the prosperity of the times. The house was later moved 18 feet north to permit Lamboll Street to be straightened.

O'DONNELL'S FOLLY, 21 KING STREET. Patrick O'Donnell was a builder from Galway, Ireland, who began this house in 1852 for his intended bride. By the time he finished it, she had married someone else, so he lived here alone. Thomas McGahan, another owner, whose wife's family had escaped the 1795 slave revolt in Santa Domingo, was Margaret Mitchell's cousin; she patterned Melanie after McGahan's wife.

MILES BREWTON HOUSE, 27 KING STREET. Completed in 1769 for Miles Brewton, a businessman, this house has been described as "the finest of American town houses" and "one of the finest . . . in the 13 original colonies." A Londoner, Ezra Waite, was the builder and carver. It cost 8,000 British pounds. During the British occupation of 1781–1782, it was the headquarters of Sir Henry Clinton and Lords Rawdon and Cornwallis. Miles Brewton and his family had been lost at sea, and his sister Rebecca Brewton Motte and her daughters lived there. Someone carved a likeness of Clinton and a ship into a marble mantle. A portrait of Miles Brewton by Sir Joshua Reynolds had a bayonet thrust through it. These insults are still in evidence. During the occupation by federal troops in 1865, it was the headquarters of Generals Hatch and Meade. In 1883, the house had passed from Miles Brewton to his sister to Col. William Alston, who married Mrs. Motte's daughter, to their daughter, Mrs. William Bull Pringle. It is still in the hands of descendants. (George Johnson.)

MILES BREWTON'S BALLROOM, 27 KING STREET. The second floor ballroom extends the width of the house and retains its elegant carvings and moldings. The Waterford chandelier was designed for the room. Most of the original outbuildings are still on the property. Because the military commanders occupied the house, there was less vandalism to it than to less protected homes.

YEADON HOUSE, 39 KING STREET. Richard Yeadon, a proprietor of the *Charleston Daily Courier*, built this house c. 1847. He was married to the daughter of John Lining, and they had no children. He gave this house as a wedding gift to his niece, Louisa Clifford Smith, who married Henry T. Thompson Jr. It was seriously damaged in the earthquake of 1886 and subsequently remodeled extensively.

PRUE HOUSE, 41 KING STREET. John Prue, husband of Sarah Townsend, built this house between 1746 and 1772. He was a carpenter with enough appreciation for education that he bequeathed this house to the "proposed college." The College of Charleston was chartered in 1785, so this was one of its first and most generous gifts.

McKEE HOUSE, 44 KING STREET. This was one of the houses that was built and owned by John McKee, who lived in Bedon's Alley. He was a successful brickmason who invested in real estate. This brick single house was built around 1796 and bequeathed to the Methodist Episcopal Church.

WEBB HOUSE, 46 KING STREET. This house was built around 1851 by Walter Webb, a florist, who grew his flowers in elaborate gardens. It has a slate roof. A car crashed into the first level of the house about 1930, leading to extensive remodeling. After Hurricane Hugo in 1989, roofers had to be imported to replace the slate and tile roofs that had been damaged.

COWAN-DILL HOUSE, 50 KING STREET. Built before 1729, this is a single house with no central hall. It is two rooms deep with the stairs rising from the back room. John Cowan built it and sold it to the Dill family, who occupied it from 1758 to 1848. This house also has the address of 6 Price's Alley. The alley is a narrow cut-through to Meeting Street.

WELLS HOUSE, 52 KING STREET. The trajectory of a cannonball can be traced through the timbers of this house, built about 1730 by Edgar Wells. Dr. George Hahnbaum, founder of the Medical Society of South Carolina, occupied the house in the 1780s. He came to South Carolina as the physician to the German Fuseliers who fought with the British in the Revolutionary War.

GRIMKE HOUSE, 55 KING STREET. Frederick Grimke built this as a double tenement *c.* 1762. This was an influential and interesting family. Frederick's daughter, Elizabeth, married John Rutledge. The artist Charles Fraser's mother was a Grimke; John Grimke took his mother's maiden name of Drayton to inherit Magnolia Plantation. Sarah and Angelina Grimke fled the state and advocated for women's rights and against slavery.

STUART HOUSE, 106 TRADD STREET. Taking a left on Tradd Street leads travelers to this nationally important house. Col. John Stuart, the Royal Commissioner for Indian Affairs, built it before 1772. The property was confiscated because he was a Tory, having taken the side of the British in the Revolution. Francis Marion supposedly broke his leg leaping from a second floor window during a party, enabling him to escape capture by the British when they occupied the city in 1780. The house itself has fine Georgian woodwork. The drawing room woodwork is a replication because the original was sold to the Minneapolis Museum of Art. A model was made of the room by Robert N.S. Whitelaw and is on display in the Charleston Museum. The octagonal wing and the piazza were added by a later owner.

WHITE HOUSE, 4 ORANGE STREET.
Proceed up Orange Street, named for an orange grove once planted there, to Broad. Before 1774, Blake Seay White built this home with an outstanding Georgian interior that remains unchanged. It was purchased in 1777 by a Tory who had it confiscated after the Revolutionary War. Blake was the grandfather of Edward Brickell White, the architect.

RIVERS HOUSE, 7 ORANGE STREET.
Alexander Petrie built this house between 1747 and 1770 and sold the surrounding lots. One was bought by Amy, "a free woman of color." The house is built of cypress and heart pine. It once had a system of bells with a different tone for each room to call the servants. M. Rutledge Rivers purchased it in 1913, and his descendants still live here.

GILMAN HOUSE, 9–11 ORANGE STREET. This 1770 house is a double tenement that has been converted to a single family home. Dr. Samuel Gilman, the minister of the Unitarian Church, lived in number 11 with his wife, Caroline Howard Gilman. She was an accomplished writer of tales, sketches, and poems and published the first children's newspaper. Two of her leather-bound books recently sold on eBay.

JOHN RUTLEDGE HOUSE, 116 BROAD STREET. This house is across Broad Street from Orange. John Rutledge built it about 1763 for his bride, Elizabeth Grimke. Rutledge represented South Carolina at the Continental Congress and the Constitutional Convention. He was the "dictator" and governor of South Carolina from 1776 to 1782. When the British occupied Charleston, someone asked where the capital of South Carolina was and was told "where ever John Rutledge's carriage is."

IRONWORK, 116 BROAD STREET. Thomas Norman Gadsden bought the house in 1853 and added the ironwork, attributed to Christopher Werner. Notice the palmetto tree and eagle. President Taft spent weekends here when it was owned by Robert Goodwyn Rhett, mayor of Charleston. It is said that Rhett's butler, William Deas, invented she crab soup here. The house is now a bed and breakfast.

EDWARD RUTLEDGE HOUSE, 117 BROAD STREET. To your left as you exit Orange Street stands the house of Edward Rutledge, John's brother, who was the youngest signer of the Declaration of Independence. Though opposed to independence, he became an officer in the militia and was imprisoned in St. Augustine. The house was built about 1760 by James Laurens, the brother of Henry Laurens, president of the Continental Congress.

PINCKNEY HOUSE, 114 BROAD STREET. This house was begun in 1790 by Ralph Izard, whose portrait is in this book, but he died during the construction. Col. Thomas Pinckney, the husband of Elizabeth Izard, Ralph's daughter, bought it still unfinished in 1829. President Jefferson Davis visited Beauregard here in 1863. In 1866, the property was sold to the Roman Catholic Bishop of Charleston, and his successors have lived here since. (George Johnson.)

POINSETT HOUSE, 110 BROAD STREET. Built by William Harvey, a butcher, c. 1728, this house was sold several times and purchased by Joel Roberts Poinsett in 1837. President James Monroe attended one of Poinsett's famous breakfasts when he visited Charleston in 1819. Poinsett served in Congress, as minister to Mexico, and as United States Secretary of War. The Poinsettia plant is named for him.

LINING HOUSE, 106 BROAD STREET. Built before 1715, this was the home of Dr. John Lining through his wife's father, Charles Hill. Dr. Lining came from Scotland in 1737 at the age of 22 and made the first documented weather observations using scientific equipment in the United States. He published papers on that and metabolism in European journals. He also corresponded with Benjamin Franklin and duplicated his experiments in electricity.

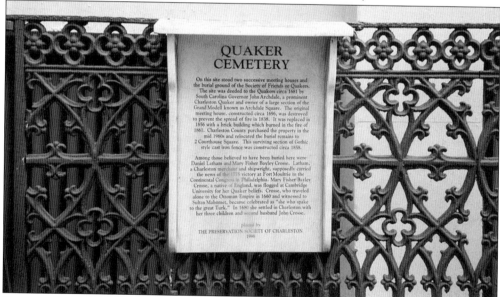

COUNTY PARKING GARAGE, 136 KING STREET. Go left and proceed up King Street. This garage is built on the site of three Quaker meeting houses. The property was deeded to the group by Gov. John Archdale, who was a Quaker. Daniel Latham, who rode on horseback to Philadelphia to deliver the news of General Moultrie's victory at Sullivan's Island in 1776, was buried here. His grave was moved to Court House Square.

CAROLINA RIFLES ARMORY, 158–160 KING STREET. After the Civil War, veterans formed "Rifle Clubs" because military units were banned and there was distrust of the federal troops. These were semi-private groups that became military units after the U.S. troops left in 1878. The unit that owned this was organized in 1869 and purchased the building in 1888. It is now part of the Library Society.

CHARLESTON LIBRARY SOCIETY, 164 KING STREET. The Library Society was formed in 1748 by gentlemen who sought to "save their descendants from sinking into savagery." The founders included nine merchants, two lawyers, a schoolmaster, a peruke-maker, a physician, and two planters. They purchased books and scientific instruments, had an exhibition on electricity in 1767, and took the first steps in founding the College of Charleston.

ENSTON BUILDING, 171–173 KING STREET. Hannah Enston, widow of William, built this around 1865 with two stores below and two residences above. Earl Mazo, biographer of Nixon, grew up here above his father's grocery store. William Enston endowed a home for the elderly (ages 45–75) at his death in 1860. The cottages were built in 1887 at 900 King Street.

BIRLANT'S CORNER. 187–191 KING STREET. Built by William Enston around 1850, this site has been the home of Birlant's Antiques since 1929. It has a granite front and is built in the Tudor Gothic Revival style. This was the first of the many antiques stores that are found on this block. The Riviera Theater is just up King Street on your left.

Tour Three

ANSONBOROUGH TOUR

Hasell, Anson, Society, Wentworth, Laurens, George, and Glebe Streets, a Detour to Bull Street, and the College of Charleston

In *This is Charleston,* Sam Stoney said, "When the Greek Revival was at its height, one of Charleston's calamitous fires cleared a space for it." He was referring to the fire of 1838, which decimated the town's first suburb, Ansonborough, where some of the city's best Greek Revival houses are found. It was laid out by Lord Adm. George Anson in 1745 on property he won from Thomas Gadsden, father of Christopher Gadsden, in a card game. Anson was a young Virginian serving in the British Navy patrolling the Charleston waters. He went on to circumnavigate the globe and become knighted for his naval service. He named the streets George, Anson, Centurion, Squirrel, and Scarborough, for himself and for his ships. Only George and Anson Streets have retained their names. In the 1950s, this area had degenerated into low-income housing with seven or eight families living in each of these houses. The reclamation project set a standard for such projects worldwide. The tour will proceed straight up Anson Street with the crossing streets described in the order that they appear. Excursions down these crossing streets are encouraged.

MAP, 1872. This map was published by C.N. Drie in 1872. (Library of Congress Map Collection.)

Kahal Kadosh Beth Elohim Synagogue, 90 Hasell Street. Exit Charleston Place on the parking garage side and you will be on Hasell Street. Directly across Hasell at number 90 is the Kahal Kadosh Beth Elohim Synagogue. Minutes of a 1695 council meeting state that some Florida Native Americans came to Charleston to trade, and they were able to do so because they had a Jew to interpret. That was possible because the Jew was a Sephardic from Spain and the Native Americans had traded with the Spanish in Florida. By 1749, they had formed a congregation, and the first synagogue was built in 1792. It burned in the fire of 1838 and was replaced by this Greek Revival building in 1840. The wrought-iron fence dates from the original. This is the second oldest synagogue in the United States and the oldest in continuous use. There is a museum of South Carolina Jewish history in the rear. This congregation began the Reform Judaism movement and installed an organ in the new building, becoming the first congregation in the United States to have one.

INTERIOR OF BETH ELOHIM, 90 HASELL STREET. The dark wood used in the interior is mahogany imported from Santo Domingo. It has a coffered dome set into a vaulted ceiling that can be seen in the photograph and features magnificent hand carving. The Charleston Preservation Society presented its Carolopolis Award for 2003 to this building.

ST. MARY'S ROMAN CATHOLIC CHURCH, 95 HASELL STREET. The church to your left replaced one that burned in 1828. The congregation was established in 1788 and consisted mostly of Irishmen and the French Santo Domingan refugees. Their first priest was from Ireland, but the church records were kept in French until 1822. The interior has paintings on the ceiling and walls painted in Rome by Caesare Porta.

86 Hasell Street. Maj. Anthony Toomer built this house *c.* 1797. Governor Lyttleton in 1759 raised a force to fight the Cherokees who were harassing the upcountry settlers. Toomer was a major in that force called the Charleston Ancient Battalion of Artillery, affectionately known as the "Old Bats"; it became the forerunner of South Carolina's Revolutionary Army and remained a social club into the 20th century.

66 Hasell Street. Walk across Meeting Street at the light and proceed down Hasell Street. This is the first house on your left. Originally a one-story structure, this was built in 1839 as a lecture hall for the Third Presbyterian Church. In 1872, it became Benjamin Lazarus's warehouse, and in 1896, a second story was added and it became Mrs. Florence Gadsden Smyth's home.

64 HASELL STREET. This property, formerly a part of the Rhett Plantation, was purchased by Benjamin F. Smith, who built this house *c.* 1843. Smith was a building supply merchant who embellished this Greek Revival house with the most elaborate ornamentation, including Tower-of-the-Winds pilasters flanking the doors and windows and fancy ironwork. It is now the Jasmine House Inn.

60 HASELL STREET. The pillars across the front of this house give it an old plantation house feel, making the Egyptian details more startling. It was built in the Italianate style by George N. Reynolds *c.* 1847. The iron-faced sitting porches on the first and second floors are an interesting innovation.

COL. WILLIAM RHETT HOUSE, 54 HASELL STREET. This is one of the oldest houses in Charleston, built between 1711 and 1722 by Col. William Rhett, who captured the pirate Stede Bonnet. Rhett was born de Raedt in the Netherlands and aided Charles II in his exile, accompanying Charles to England when he assumed the throne. He was made Receiver-General of the Lords Proprietors in South Carolina. (George Johnson.)

INTERIOR OF 54 HASELL STREET. The interior has early Georgian paneling and plaster decorations but was remodeled in the Adamesque style *c.* 1800. Wade Hampton III, Civil War general, United States senator, and South Carolina governor, was born here in 1818. He was said to own the most land in the South at the beginning of the Civil War. His plantations were in Richland County, South Carolina.

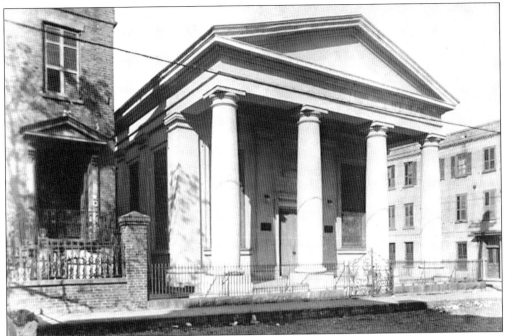

ST. JOHANNES EVANGELICAL LUTHERAN CHURCH, 48 HASELL STREET. This church was built by the St. Matthews Lutheran congregation in 1841, and when they built the new church on King Street in 1872, this was sold to the Salem Baptist Church, an African-American congregation. St. Johannes Evangelical Lutheran purchased it in 1878 and still uses it. Services were conducted in German until 1924. (George Johnson.)

44 HASELL STREET. James M. Stocker, a merchant, built this Greek Revival house between 1840 and 1849, when he sold it to John Charles Blum. It has an interesting floor plan with no central stair; the stairs are located behind a suite of rooms. This style is more often found in New Orleans.

25 ANSON STREET. The row of single houses (11–25) was built by Isaac A. Goldsmith as tenements in 1894. He was a dentist, industrialist, and real estate developer. The houses were occupied by Irish, German, and Jewish families. There were distilleries on this site in 1788. It was called Goldsmith's Row. The child in the picture lived in the neighborhood.

THE PALMETTO FIRE COMPANY HALL, 27 ANSON STREET. Proceed up Anson Street. A volunteer firefighting unit built this Italianate structure in 1850 using Edward C. Jones as the architect. When it was converted into apartments in the 1940s, the fire engine entrance was enclosed with a pair of windows. The change makes an interesting facade.

110

46 ANSON STREET. This U-shaped complex was built to accommodate the house and outbuildings on a shallow lot. Thomas Wallace, a dry goods merchant, built it before 1853. Because of the necessity of separate kitchens and other dependencies, small lots sometimes made building designs interesting. This shape is more common in today's suburb than it was when this was built.

22–24 WENTWORTH STREET. To the right on Wentworth Street is the home of Francis Quinlan McHugh, an attorney. It was a duplex with the west side serving as his home. He used a "fire loan" from the Bank of the State of South Carolina, which probably means he owned a previous house on the site. It became a single family home when it was renovated c. 1969.

ST. ANDREW'S LUTHERAN CHURCH, 43 WENTWORTH STREET. This church is to the left on Wentworth Street. The original church on this site was built by a Methodist group that split from the Methodist Episcopal Church in a dispute over the seating of African-American members. This church, built after the fire, was damaged in the Civil War and became the home of a combined Lutheran congregation.

60 ANSON STREET. This is one of several houses in the neighborhood built by members of the Venning family, planters of Christ Church Parish. It was built by R.M. Venning, a planter and factor, c. 1851 in an L shape because of the narrowness of the lot. In the renovation, the floor boards from the first level were used as paneling in the upstairs sitting room.

49–51 SOCIETY STREET. To the left on Society Street is the convent of the Oblate Sisters of Charity. It was built in 1838 by Edward Roach, whose son married the daughter of William Gilmore Simms, the historian. In 1883, the Roman Catholic Church established St. Peter's Colored School here and added the eastern wing. Several charitable groups established schools for the freed slaves after the Civil War.

CHARLESTON HIGH SCHOOL, 55 SOCIETY STREET. This was the city's high school when it was built about 1842. Edward Brickell White was the architect. The Corinthian capitals, made in New England, were lost in the 1886 earthquake and not restored until after 1985. The school had moved in 1881, so the building was little used until it was renovated and made into apartments in 1983.

ST. STEPHEN'S EPISCOPAL CHURCH, 67 ANSON STREET. This church was built in 1835 and 1836 for Episcopalians who could not afford to purchase or rent pews in the other Episcopal churches. It was designed by Henry Horlbeck and built with bricks from his brickyard at Boone Hall Plantation. The original St. Stephen's Chapel was the first Episcopal church in the United States to offer free pews.

71 ANSON STREET. Mary Legare Doughty, wife of Thomas, inherited this property from her father, Daniel Legare, who built the house at 79 Anson. She and Thomas built this Adamesque house c. 1806 with a gabled pavilion on the garden side. This was the first house renovated in the Ansonborough Rehabilitation Project in 1959 by a family sponsored by the Historic Charleston Foundation. (George Johnson.)

61 LAURENS STREET. James Mckie built this house about 1800 on the site of the Gaillard Auditorium. The houses to be displaced by the auditorium were evaluated, and this one and number 39 were chosen to be moved, replacing houses that were not salvageable. Speaking of the whole project, someone wise said, "It's amazing what you can accomplish when you don't care who you make mad."

57 LAURENS STREET. This house was built *c.* 1836 of black cypress in the Greek Revival style by Thomas Porcher. His daughter married Pierre G. Stoney, and the house remained in that family into the 20th century. Samuel Gaillard Stoney in *This is Charleston* lists 53, 55, and 57 Laurens Street as valuable. Subsequent owners have installed an outstanding garden with a reflecting pool.

55 LAURENS STREET. James Jervey built this substantial house *c.* 1818. Powder kegs were reportedly placed in the basement during the fire of 1838 to blow up the house if necessary. Luckily, the fire went in the other direction, and this house and its immediate neighbors were saved. That is what gives Laurens Street its ambiance.

75 ANSON STREET. Joseph Legare built this house *c.* 1800, but Benjamin J. Howland made many changes to it when he bought it in 1838. It was called the "white elephant" of the Ansonborough Project because no one would buy it, so the new owner who bought it in 1974 painted it "elephant grey." The restoration project that owner undertook included removing the 1838 additions except for the curving stair.

79 ANSON STREET. Daniel Legare, father of Joseph, finished this house about 1760. This is the oldest surviving house of the Colonial Ansonborough suburb. Daniel was a Huguenot planter in Christ Church Parish, and this was built as his town house. His brother, Soloman, was a silversmith for whom Legare Street is named. Samuel Stoney lists 71, 75, 79, 114, and 116 Anson Street as valuable.

82 ANSON STREET. Josiah Smith, a merchant, built this house for his spinster daughter, Mary Smith, *c.* 1799, in hopes of attracting her a suitor. For some reason, she remained a spinster and lived here until she died. The current owner says that she haunts one room on the fourth floor. Jingling keys are heard and people have felt someone pressing on them as they slept.

7 GEORGE STREET. The walk continues left up George Street. This stuccoed brick single house was built about 1813 for Mary, the unmarried daughter of William Scott and Elizabeth Legare, on property that belonged to her grandfather, Daniel Legare. She lived here until her death in 1849. It is two and a half stories over a high basement.

8 GEORGE STREET. This house was built by Robert Daniell between 1787 and 1791, when it conveyed from his estate to his daughter, Sarah, wife of Jonathan Lawrence. It has Palladian windows in the end gables and handsome architectural details inside. The details of the piazza railings are more ornate than most from this period. The use of the upper rail is also quite unusual for that time.

14 George Street. Fourteen George was built by Mrs. Frances Motte Middleton Pinckney as her home in 1797. A daughter of Rebecca Brewton Motte, Frances hid in the attic of 27 King Street during the British occupation. Thomas Pinckney, son of Chief Justice Charles Pinckney and his wife, Eliza Lucas, was Frances's second husband.

Interior, 14 George Street. The house was built in a cruciform plan with polygonal bays in the front and back. The interior is in the Regency style with elaborate hand-carved woodwork throughout. The chandelier in this photograph is original. Mrs. Pinckney's son, John Middleton, inherited the house in 1822, but it eventually devolved to become offices. It is now the headquarters for the Spoleto Festival U.S.A.

287 MEETING STREET. As you cross Meeting Street at George, this building is on your left. Built in 1870 in the Gothic Revival style as the Deutsche Freundschafts Bund Hall, it has been used as a Masonic Temple. It is now headquarters for the Washington Light Infantry, organized in 1807. The gates were designed by Albert Simons in the 1950s.

32 GEORGE STREET. This house was built for Elizabeth Robinson, who rented it to Peter Freneau, a journalist and shipowner, from 1801. He was a Huguenot who came from New Jersey in 1782 to co-edit the *City Gazette and Daily Advertiser.* He served as secretary of state and managed Jefferson's presidential campaign in South Carolina. He never purchased the house but lived there until he died in 1813.

58 GEORGE STREET. Barnard Elliott, a planter, built this house about 1803. The interior woodwork was salvaged from a house at 26 George that was demolished. It is now a part of the College of Charleston campus, as are most of the buildings in this area. Rather than tear down the surrounding houses, the college has chosen to adapt them.

TOWELL LIBRARY, COLLEGE OF CHARLESTON, 66 GEORGE STREET. This Italianate building was designed by George E. Walker and completed in 1856. The floor plan is patterned after Robert Mills's plan for South Carolina College and Latrobe's plan for the Library of Congress. The main room is two stories high with encircling galleries. The college's newest library will open in 2005 on the corner of Coming and Calhoun Streets.

HARRISON RANDOLPH HALL, COLLEGE OF CHARLESTON, 66 GEORGE STREET. In 1770, Benjamin Smith bequeathed 1,000 pounds to found a local college, but it took until 1785 for an Act of the General Assembly to establish the college and until 1790 for it to actually open. Randolph Hall was built in 1826. It became a municipal college in 1837, the oldest in the United States. In 1949, it became private, and then in 1970, it became a state institution. Perhaps because it had a strenuous entrance examination or perhaps because it had no football team, it was thought of as an intellectual school. Contributing to that reputation was the fact that until 1970, Latin or Greek was required to receive a Bachelor of Arts degree. There are still people around with Bachelor of Science degrees in history. Student life and graduations center on the cistern in front of Randolph Hall.

WILLIAM BLACKLOCK HOUSE, 18 BULL STREET. A short detour going right on Coming Street to the next corner will take you to one of the most important Adamesque houses in the United States. Built in 1800, the house features a large lunette in the pediment and delicate tracery in the fan light. It was designated a National Historic Landmark in 1974 and houses the College of Charleston Club. (George Johnson.)

BLACKLOCK INTERIOR, 18 BULL STREET. This is a 1940 photograph of the second-floor parlor. The chandelier is original and has not been electrified. The depth shown in the window surround represents the thickness of the walls throughout the house. The house also features a free-standing staircase with a coved decorative ceiling. Walk back to George Street and enter Glebe Street across from Randolph Hall.

20 GLEBE STREET. The glebe land was donated to the Episcopal Church by Affra Harleston Coming in 1698. It was divided into lots with Glebe Street cut through in 1797. The people who built these houses leased the land for 31 years with the option of renewing. If the tenant did not renew the lease, he could donate the house or remove it. This is now the faculty house.

7 GLEBE STREET. All of the houses on Glebe appear on a map dated 1855 and are now part of the college except for number 7. This is the Mount Zion African Methodist Episcopal Church, built in 1847 and designed by Francis D. Lee, who was a recent graduate of the college. The interior has much in common with St. Michael's, including boxed pews and arched windows.

6 GLEBE STREET. This house was built in 1770 as the parsonage of St. Phillips Church and now serves as the home of the president of the College of Charleston. It was the home of Rev. Robert Smith, who was the first president of the college and South Carolina's first Episcopal bishop. Classes met here until classrooms could be built. The Georgian interior is excellent.

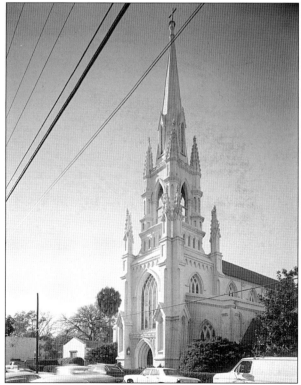

GRACE EPISCOPAL CHURCH, 100 WENTWORTH STREET. This Gothic Revival church was built in 1847. It was designed by Edward Brickell White. During the Civil War occupation, the minister, Rev. Dr. Charles Cotesworth Pinckney, was ordered to pray for the president of the United States while federal soldiers watched. He complied, saying he knew of no one who needed praying for more. This church is known for its music program.

92 WENTWORTH STREET. The tour proceeds left on Wentworth Street toward King Street. This house, built around 1850, was totally reinvented by Jacob Knobeloch, a flour dealer, who purchased it in 1881. He turned the house sideways to the street and replaced the siding. He also added a mansard roof, new piazza elements, and a new entrance door. The interior, however, retains the plaster and woodwork of the 1850s.

87–89 WENTWORTH STREET. This double tenement was built between 1770, when the glebe lands were divided, and 1788, when it appears on a fire insurance map. St. Michael's Church retained title to the land until 1953. The Bermuda stone structures share one wall and the chimneys. Number 87 was remodeled in the late 19th century, but number 89 retains its 18th-century appearance.

270 King Street. This Tudor Gothic building was built in 1871 and 1872 as the Orange Lodge Number 14 of the Ancient Free Masons. John Henry Devereaux, though a Roman Catholic, joined the Masons so it could be said that it was built by a member of the organization. Arthur Mazyck, in *Charleston 1883*, describes it as an "English cathedral turned inside out."

King Street at Night. This photograph was taken around 1910 and shows that the commercial area of King Street had electric lights installed. The paving looks like brick, and there are trolley tracks in the street. The kiosk seen at the left was located very near the corner of King and Beaufain Street, so this view corresponds to your view as you walk.

KING STREET. This *c.* 1880s photograph was taken near where Beaufain Street crosses King and faces north. The horse buggies are parked by dropping a weight from the bit in the horse's mouth. Hasell Street is on your left and the parking garage entrance to Charleston Place is on your right halfway down Hasell. I hope this has been an enjoyable adventure. Writing it certainly was for me. (South Carolina Historical Association.)